NFL TEAMS

BY LARRY MACK

THE TAMPA BAY BUCCANEERS STORY

BELLWETHER MEDIA · MINNEAPOLIS, MN

Are you ready to take it to the extreme? Torque books thrust you into the action-packed world of sports, vehicles, mystery, and adventure. These books may include dirt, smoke, fire, and chilling tales. **WARNING**: read at your own risk.

This edition first published in 2017 by Bellwether Media, Inc.

Library of Congress Cataloging-in-Publication Data

Names: Mack, Larry, author.
Title: The Tampa Bay Buccaneers Story / by Larry Mack.
Description: Minneapolis, MN : Bellwether Media, Inc., 2017. | Series: Torque: NFL Teams | Includes bibliographical references and index.
Identifiers: LCCN 2015047959 | ISBN 9781626173842 (hardcover : alk. paper)
Subjects: LCSH: Tampa Bay Buccaneers (Football team)–History–Juvenile literature.
Classification: LCC GV956.T35 M34 2017 | DDC 796.332/640975965–dc23
LC record available at http://lccn.loc.gov/2015047959

Printed in the United States of America, North Mankato, MN.

TABLE OF CONTENTS

The Tampa Bay Buccaneers need to beat the Atlanta Falcons. A win today will make them **division** champions for the 2007 season.

Jeff Garcia

A TEAM FIRST

With his return, Spurlock became the first Buc to score a touchdown on a kickoff!

The Falcons kick the ball to the Bucs. **Wide receiver** Micheal Spurlock catches the kick. He speeds up the field. He cuts quickly to the right. Then he races up the sideline. Spurlock scores!

Ronde Barber

The touchdown puts the Bucs up 13 to 3. It also gives the Bucs a boost. They score 24 more points and win 37 to 3.

What a way for Bucs fans to spend the afternoon! Their team has easily defeated a main **rival**. They are also headed to the **playoffs**!

SCORING TERMS

END ZONE

the area at each end of a football field; a team scores by entering the opponent's end zone with the football.

EXTRA POINT

a score that occurs when a kicker kicks the ball between the opponent's goal posts after a touchdown is scored; 1 point.

FIELD GOAL

a score that occurs when a kicker kicks the ball between the opponent's goal posts; 3 points.

SAFETY

a score that occurs when a player on offense is tackled behind his own goal line; 2 points for defense.

TOUCHDOWN

a score that occurs when a team crosses into its opponent's end zone with the football; 6 points.

TWO-POINT CONVERSION

a score that occurs when a team crosses into its opponent's end zone with the football after scoring a touchdown; 2 points.

FROM WORST TO FIRST

The Tampa Bay Buccaneers made it to the top of the National Football League (NFL) from the bottom. In their first season, the Bucs had zero wins.

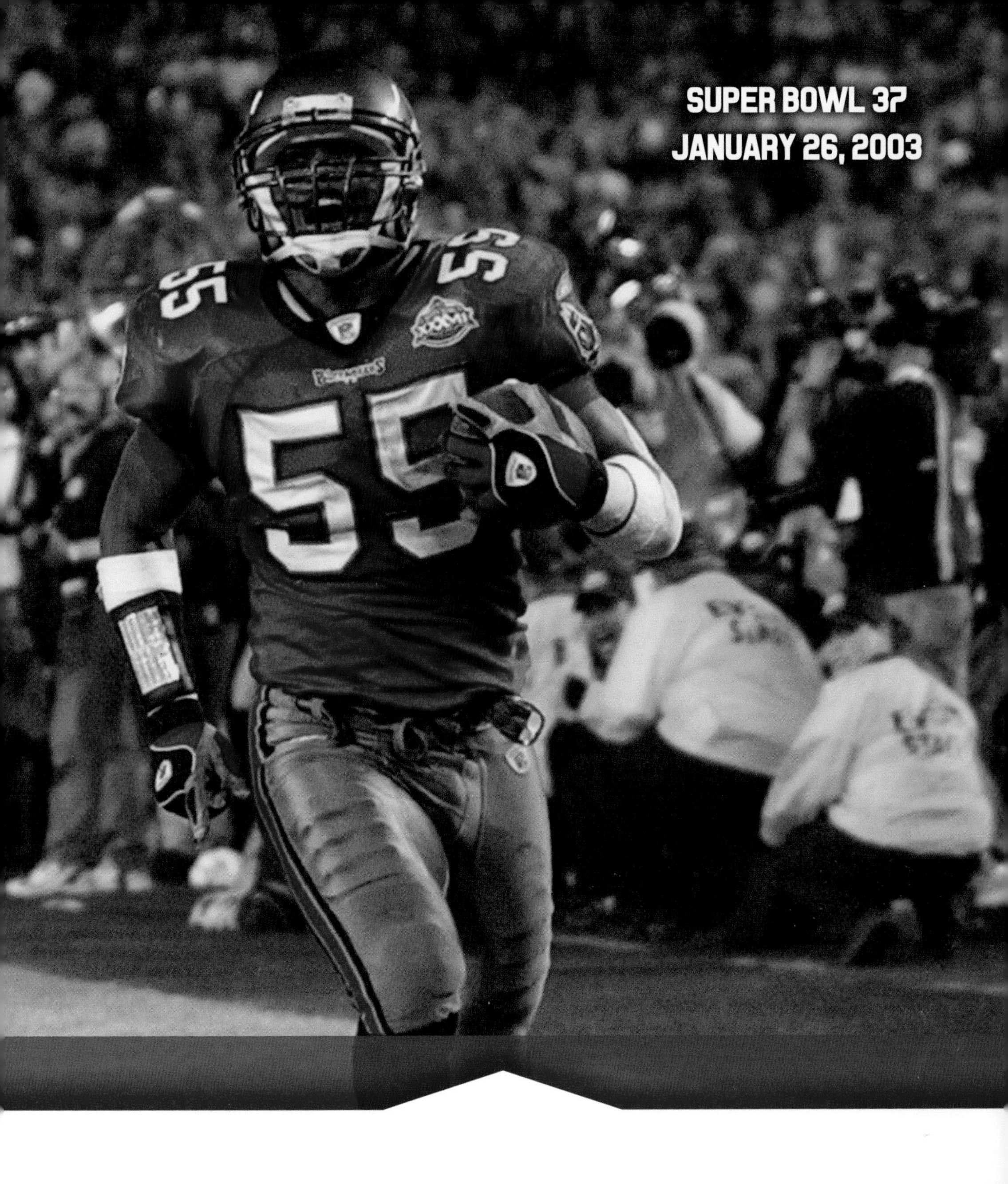

But this beginning did not sink the team's spirit. In 2003, the Bucs made it to **Super Bowl** 37. They beat the Oakland Raiders 48 to 21!

RAYMOND JAMES STADIUM

The Bucs are one of three NFL teams in Florida. They play home games at Raymond James Stadium in Tampa.

The stadium is famous for its Buccaneer **Cove**. Here, a gigantic pirate ship sits above one end zone. A puppet-like parrot on the ship even talks to fans walking past!

PIRATES IN THE BAY

The Bucs' name refers to stories of pirates in Florida. Some pirates were called buccaneers.

TAMPA, FLORIDA

N
W E
S

The Bucs play in the National Football **Conference** (NFC). They are in the NFC South Division.

All of the Bucs' division rivals are in southern states. The Atlanta Falcons are in Georgia. The New Orleans Saints are in Louisiana. The Panthers play for both North and South Carolina.

NFC

NFC NORTH

CHICAGO **BEARS**

DETROIT **LIONS**

GREEN BAY **PACKERS**

MINNESOTA **VIKINGS**

NFC EAST

DALLAS **COWBOYS**

NEW YORK **GIANTS**

PHILADELPHIA **EAGLES**

WASHINGTON **REDSKINS**

NFC SOUTH

ATLANTA **FALCONS**

CAROLINA **PANTHERS**

NEW ORLEANS **SAINTS**

TAMPA BAY **BUCCANEERS**

NFC WEST

ARIZONA **CARDINALS**

LOS ANGELES **RAMS**

SAN FRANCISCO **49ERS**

SEATTLE **SEAHAWKS**

THEN TO NOW

The Bucs began as an NFL **expansion team** in 1976. In the beginning, they struggled against other teams. The Bucs lost their first 26 games.

But head coach John McKay helped the team improve. In 1979, the Bucs won more games than they lost. They also made it to the conference championship for that season!

John McKay

1979 season

FLORIDA ORANGE

The Bucs used to wear bright "Florida orange" uniforms. Today, red is the team's main color.

In 1983, another rough stretch started for the Bucs. The team had fourteen losing seasons in a row.

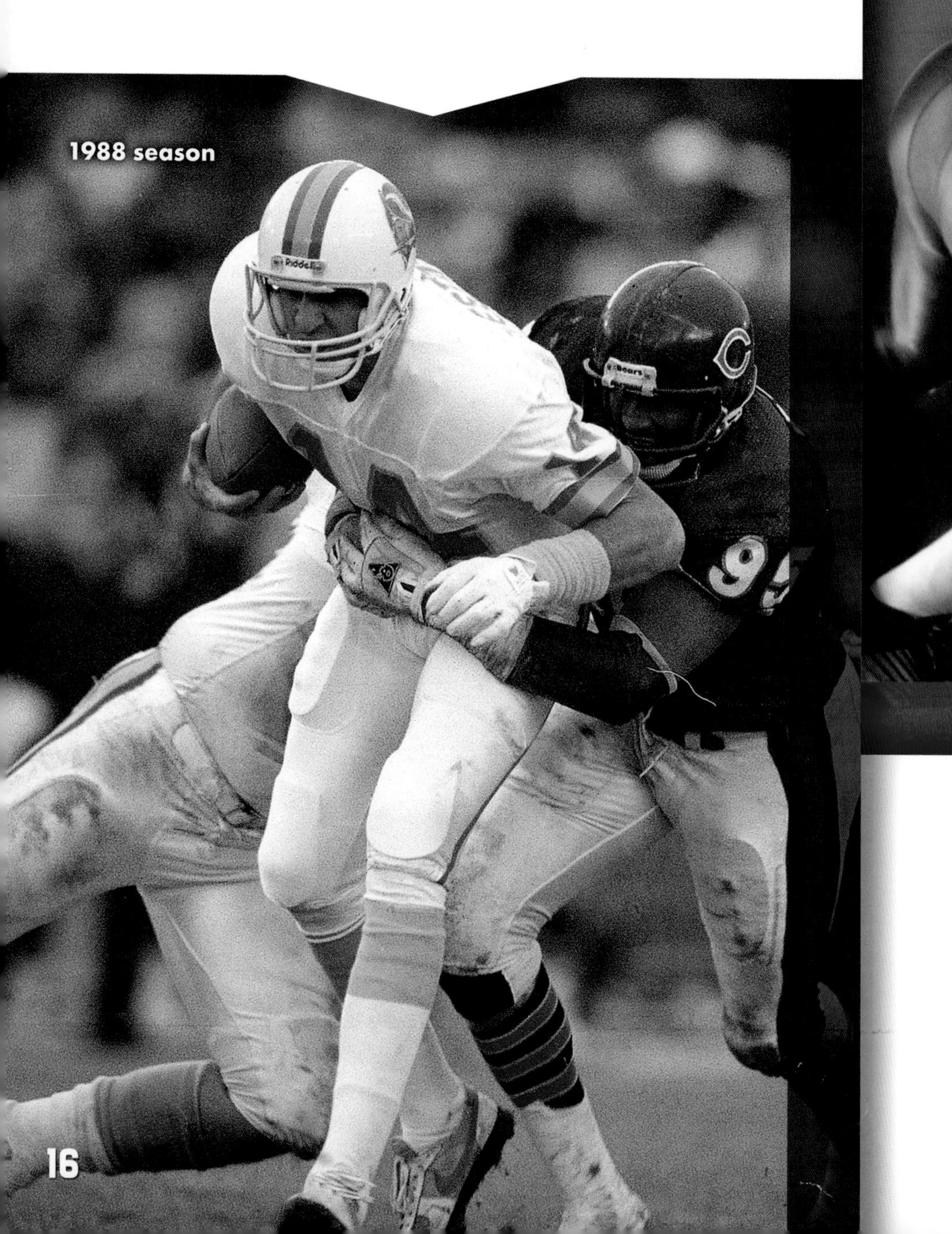

1988 season

TAKE THAT!

Coach Gruden was traded to the Bucs from the Oakland Raiders in 2002. In his first season with the Bucs, he led them to a Super Bowl win over his old team!

Then a new period began in the late 1990s. Head coach Tony Dungy built the Bucs' **defense** into a force. Following the 2002 season, Tampa Bay won Super Bowl 37 with new head coach Jon Gruden.

BUCCANEERS

TIMELINE

1976

Joined the NFL as an expansion team

1977

Won a regular-season game for the first time ever, beating the New Orleans Saints (33-14)

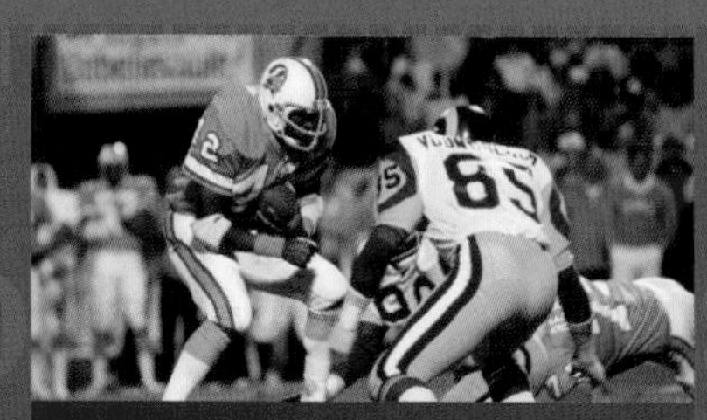

1980

Played in the NFC Championship game, but lost to the Los Angeles Rams (0-9)

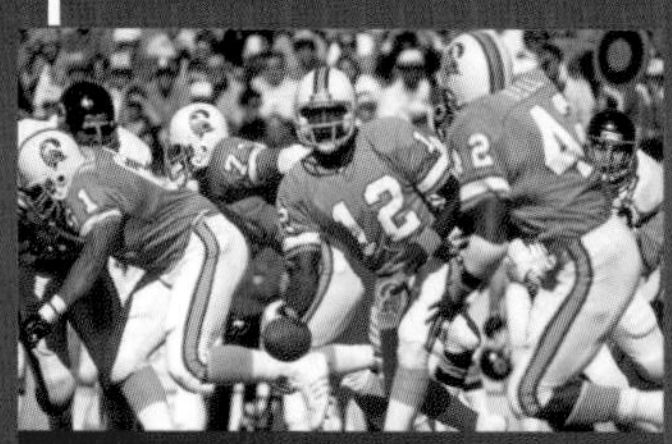

1981

Claimed their second division title

1996

Hired Tony Dungy as head coach

1998

First played at Raymond James Stadium

2000

Played in the NFC Championship game, but lost to the St. Louis Rams

6 FINAL SCORE 11

2002

Hired Jon Gruden as head coach

2003

Won Super Bowl 37, beating the Oakland Raiders

48 FINAL SCORE 21

2005

Claimed fifth division title

2007

Claimed sixth division title

Lee Roy Selmon was the Bucs' first superstar. He played **defensive end** in the early years. His skills took him to the **Pro Bowl** six times in a row!

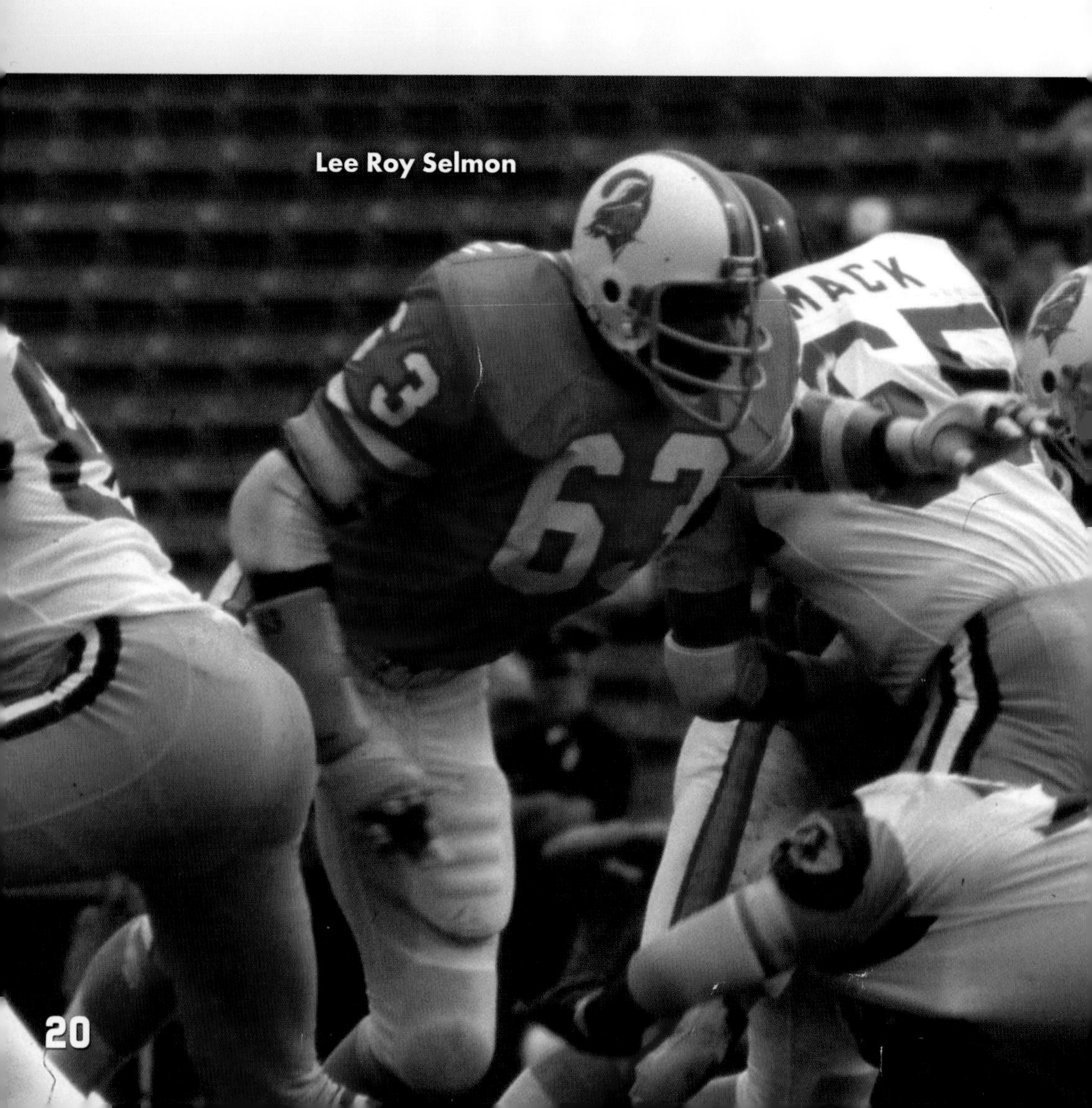

Lee Roy Selmon

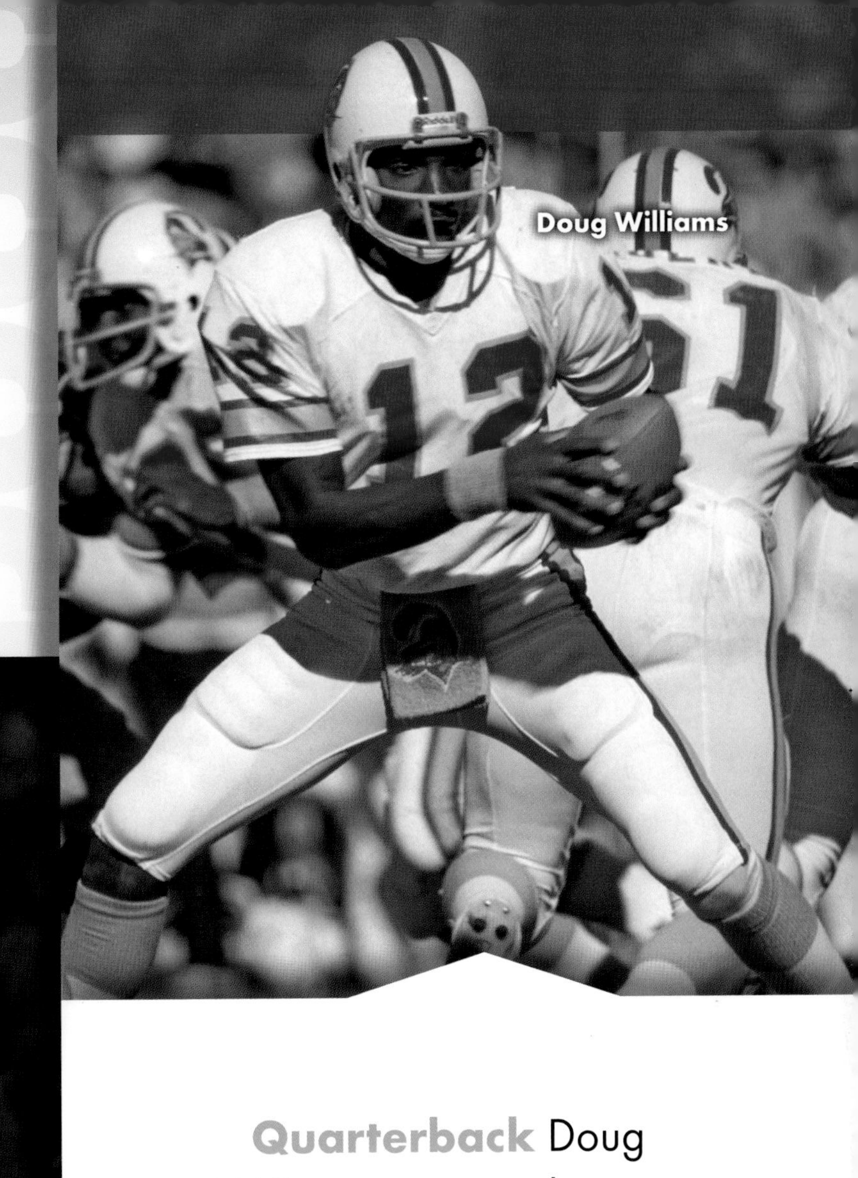

Doug Williams

Quarterback Doug Williams was another early Bucs star. Before he arrived in 1978, the team had won only two games. The next season, Williams led the team to the NFC Championship game.

In the 1990s, the Bucs became known for great defense. Tackle Warren Sapp and **linebacker** Derrick Brooks were both stars. John Lynch and Ronde Barber were great **defensive backs**.

Two current Bucs stars are **running back** Doug Martin and wide receiver Mike Evans. Both are scoring threats for the Bucs.

TEAM GREATS

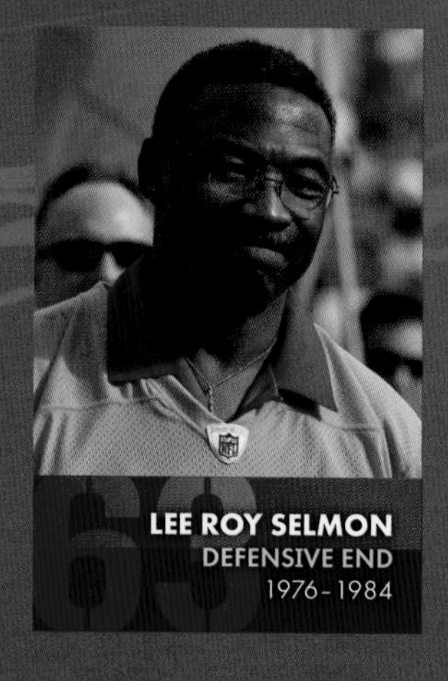

LEE ROY SELMON
DEFENSIVE END
1976-1984

DOUG WILLIAMS
QUARTERBACK
1978-1982

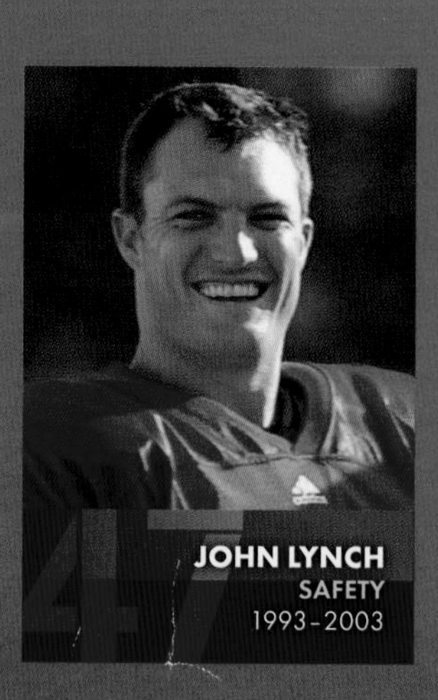

JOHN LYNCH
SAFETY
1993-2003

Mike Evans

ANOTHER TALENTED MIKE

Another Buc named Mike was a star of Super Bowl 37. Mike Alstott scored the first touchdown of that game!

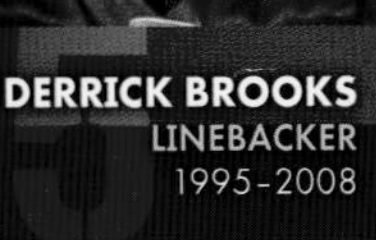

DERRICK BROOKS
LINEBACKER
1995-2008

MIKE ALSTOTT
RUNNING BACK
1996-2006

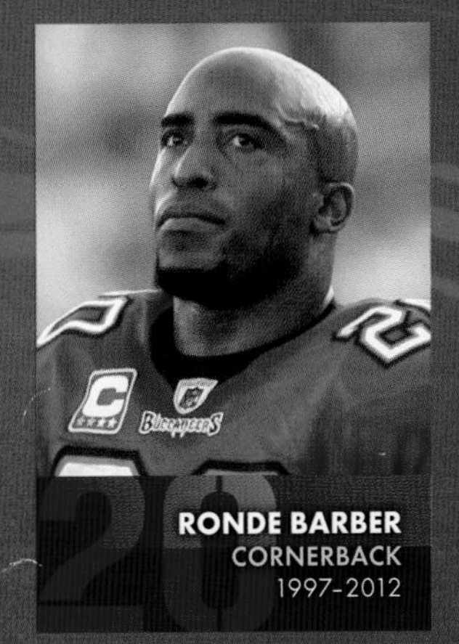

RONDE BARBER
CORNERBACK
1997-2012

FANS AND TEAM CULTURE

Bucs fans love their fun traditions. Going to a Bucs home game is a bit like going to Walt Disney World.

Team mascot, Captain Fear, visits fans outside the stadium. Inside, workers dressed as pirates greet fans. "Yo Ho," the theme song from Pirates of the Caribbean, is played.

Captain Fear

Buccaneer Cove helps fans celebrate big Tampa Bay plays on the field. Cannons on the pirate ship shoot smoke and confetti.

The cannons fire once for every point scored. One shot is also fired when the Bucs get within 20 yards of the end zone. Win or lose, every home game is a blast!

MORE ABOUT THE BUCCANEERS

Team name:
Tampa Bay Buccaneers

Team name explained:
Named for the pirates connected to the Florida area

Nickname: The Bucs

Joined NFL: 1976

Conference: NFC

Division: South

Main rivals: Atlanta Falcons, New Orleans Saints

Hometown:
Tampa, Florida

Training camp location:
One Buccaneer Place, Tampa, Florida

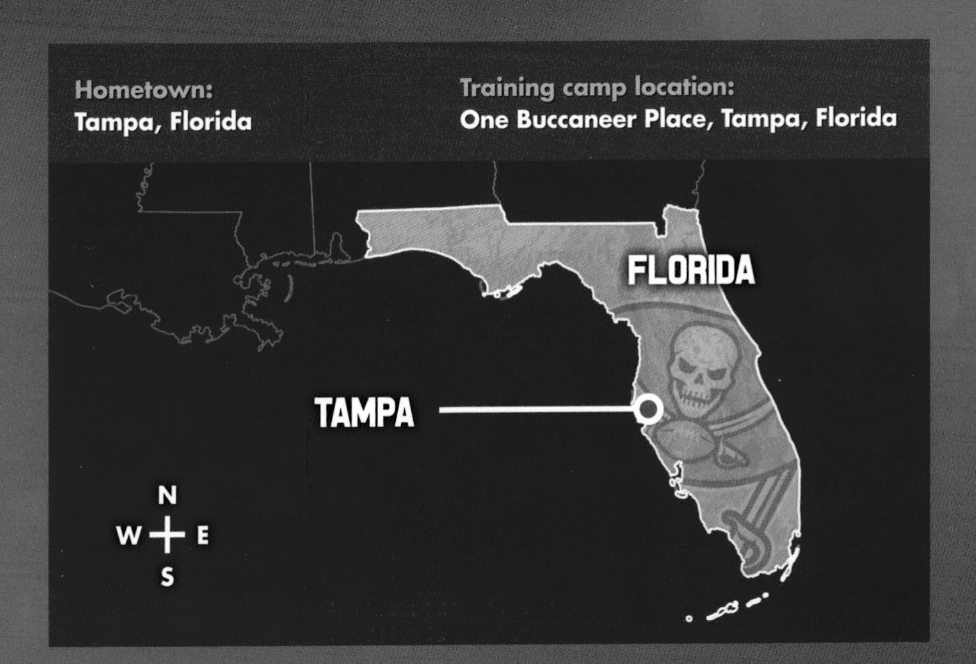

Home stadium name:
Raymond James Stadium

Stadium opened: 1998

Seats in stadium: 65,890

Logo: A red flag with skull, football, and crossed swords

Colors: Red, orange, pewter

Mascot: Captain Fear

GLOSSARY

conference—a large grouping of sports teams that often play one another

cove—a small, sheltered bay

defense—the group of players who try to stop the opposing team from scoring

defensive backs—players with the main job of stopping receivers from catching passes

defensive end—a player on defense whose job is to tackle the player with the ball

division—a small grouping of sports teams that often play one another; usually there are several divisions of teams in a conference.

expansion team—a new team added to a sports league

linebacker—a player on defense whose main job is to make tackles and stop passes; a linebacker stands just behind the defensive linemen.

playoffs—the games played after the regular NFL season is over; playoff games determine which teams play in the Super Bowl.

Pro Bowl—an all-star game played after the regular season in which the best players in the NFL face one another

quarterback—a player on offense whose main job is to throw and hand off the ball

rival—a long-standing opponent

running back—a player on offense whose main job is to run with the ball

Super Bowl—the championship game for the NFL

wide receiver—a player on offense whose main job is to catch passes from the quarterback

TO LEARN MORE

AT THE LIBRARY

Frisch, Aaron. *Tampa Bay Buccaneers.* Mankato, Minn.: Creative Education, 2014.

Frisch, Nate. *The Story of the Tampa Bay Buccaneers.* Mankato, Minn.: Creative Education, 2014.

Temple, Ramey. *Tampa Bay Buccaneers.* New York, N.Y.: AV2 by Weigl, 2015.

ON THE WEB

Learning more about the Tampa Bay Buccaneers is as easy as 1, 2, 3.

1. Go to www.factsurfer.com.
2. Enter "Tampa Bay Buccaneers" into the search box.
3. Click the "Surf" button and you will see a list of related web sites.

With factsurfer.com, finding more information is just a click away.

INDEX

The images in this book are reproduced through the courtesy of: Corbis, front cover (large, small), pp. 4-5, 8-9, 12-13, 18 (top), 19 (top), 23 (left); Scott Audette/ AP Images, pp. 5, 29 (mascot); ZUMA Press/ Alamy, pp. 6-7, 24, 25; Scott A. Miller/ ZUMA Press/ Newscom, p. 7; Birgit Tyrrell/ Alamy, pp. 10-11, 26; Scott Halleran/ Getty Images, p. 11; Deposit Photos/ Glow Images, pp. 12-13 (logos), 18-19 (logos), 28-29 (logos); NFL Photos/ AP Images, pp. 14, 20-21; Al Messerschmidt/ AP Images, pp. 15, 18 (bottom), 21, 22 (middle), 29 (stadium); John Swart/ AP Images, p. 16; Gary W. Green/ KRT/ Newscom, pp. 16-17; John Rivera/ Icon SMI/ Newscom, p. 19 (bottom); Daniel Wallace/ ZUMA Press/ Newscom, p. 22 (left); St. Petersburg Times/ ZUMA Press/ Newscom, p. 22 (right); Cathy Kapulka/ UPI/ Newscom, p. 23 (middle); Gary W. Green/ MCT/ Newscom, p. 23 (right); Phelan M. Ebenhack/ AP Images, pp. 26-27; Scott Martin/ AP Images, p. 28.